Eagle, Globe, Anchor, and Cross

By Rick White

PRESS

Copyright © 2007 by Eric White

Eagle Globe Anchor and Cross
by Eric White

Printed in the United States of America

ISBN 978-1-60266-049-6

www.xulonpress.com

To June, who never put on a uniform, but remains one of the best Marines I have ever known.

Introduction

⸺⸙⸺

W hen I became a Christian at thirty-two years of age I kept walls up between my faith and my job unnecessarily because the two seemed to have little in common. As I began to understand the need to be a Marine as though I was working for God, I realized that there has been very little written of practical help for military members. The main purpose of this book is to look at Marine Corps life from a Christian perspective. Maybe it will help someone else bring down the walls in their life and ultimately help them to love God and love their neighbor to the fullest.

I have written this book for Marines who are Christians with the expectations that you are familiar with the customs and courtesies of the Corps. If you are a Marine's parent or the member of another of the services and are puzzled by some of the references, you may find answers at www.usmc.mil. Scripture is included in the text quite often since Marines may not always have their Bibles with them.

In each chapter are references to the Marine Corps leadership traits that apply to the topic being addressed. For those unfamiliar with these traits, they are:

- bearing
- dependability
- knowledge
- initiative
- integrity
- courage
- tact
- unselfishness
- decisiveness
- justice
- judgment
- enthusiasm
- loyalty
- endurance

Table of Contents

CHAPTER 1

Uriah, the First Marine

A ll right, I admit it—I have no evidence that Uriah the Hittite was a Marine. I'm not even positive that the Old Testament Israelites had a Marine Corps. But if they had, Uriah would have been the one to inspire them to adopt Semper Fidelis as their motto. He would have made a great captain or gunny in today's Corps. Courage, honor, and commitment just welled up from his heart. In case you're not familiar with Uriah, take a look at the eleventh chapter of second Samuel in the Old Testament. Turning to that chapter you would assume that you were going to hear about King David. It is most natural to look at the life of David when we consider men of both faith and great military capability. Unfortunately, what we see of David in this instance is a terrible example of corruption and abuse of power by a leader. If we ever needed a description of the reason why "you shall not covet your neighbor's wife" is part of the Ten Commandments, we can find it here. Blinded by lust and accustomed to getting his own way, David used his position as king to have Bathsheba, another man's wife. When he found out she was pregnant he went to extraordinary lengths to cover his sin.

David and Bathsheba

In the spring, at the time when kings go off to war, David sent Joab out with the king's men and the whole Israelite army. They destroyed the Ammonites and besieged Rabbah. But David remained in Jerusalem.

One evening David got up from his bed and walked around on the roof of the palace. From the roof he saw a woman bathing. The woman was very beautiful, and David sent someone to find out about her. The man said, "Isn't this Bathsheba, the daughter of Eliam and the wife of Uriah the Hittite?" Then David sent messengers to get her. She came to him, and he slept with her. (She had purified herself from her uncleanness.) Then she went back home. The woman conceived and sent word to David, saying, "I am pregnant."

So David sent this word to Joab: "Send me Uriah the Hittite." And Joab sent him to David. When Uriah came to him, David asked him how Joab was, how the soldiers were and how the war was going. Then David said to Uriah, "Go down to your house and wash your feet." So Uriah left the palace, and a gift from the king was sent after him. But Uriah slept at the entrance to the palace with all his master's servants and did not go down to his house.

When David was told, "Uriah did not go home," he asked him, "Haven't you just come from a distance? Why didn't you go home?"

Uriah said to David, "The ark and Israel and Judah are staying in tents, and my master Joab and my lord's men are camped in the open fields. How could I go to my house to eat and drink and lie with my wife? As surely as you live, I will not do such a thing!"

Then David said to him, "Stay here one more day, and tomorrow I will send you back." So Uriah remained in Jerusalem that day and the next. At David's invitation, he ate and drank with him, and David made him drunk. But in the evening Uriah went out to sleep on his mat among his master's servants; he did not go home.

In the morning David wrote a letter to Joab and sent it with Uriah. In it he wrote, "Put Uriah in the front line where the fighting is fiercest. Then withdraw from him so he will be struck down and die."

So while Joab had the city under siege, he put Uriah at a place where he knew the strongest defenders were. When the men of the city came out and fought against Joab, some of the men in David's army fell; moreover, Uriah the Hittite died.

Joab sent David a full account of the battle. He instructed the messenger: "When you have finished giving the king this account of the battle, the king's anger may flare up, and he may ask you, 'Why did you get so close to the city to fight? Didn't you know they would shoot arrows from the wall? Who killed Abimelech son of Jerub-Besheth? Didn't a woman throw an upper millstone on him from the wall, so that he died in Thebez? Why did you get so close to the wall?' If he asks you this, then say to him, 'Also, your servant Uriah the Hittite is dead.'"

The messenger set out, and when he arrived he told David everything Joab had sent him to say. The messenger said to David, "The men overpowered us and came out against us in the open, but we drove them back to the entrance to the city gate. Then the archers shot arrows at your servants from the wall, and some of the king's men died. Moreover, your servant Uriah the Hittite is dead."

David told the messenger, "Say this to Joab: 'Don't let this upset you; the sword devours one as well as another. Press the attack against the city and destroy it.' Say this to encourage Joab."

When Uriah's wife heard that her husband was dead, she mourned for him. After the time of mourning was over, David had her brought to his house, and she became his wife and bore him a son. But the thing David had done displeased the LORD.

2 Samuel 11

In contrast to David, Bathsheba's husband Uriah displayed an incredible sense of honor. He refused to indulge in the comforts of home while the ark and the men of God were camped on the field of battle. It would have been easy to say, "The king made me do it!" He obeyed when his king told him to go to his house and wash his feet. Can you imagine the urges that he must have overcome? He had spent an extended time away in the field and then he showed up at home with a gift in hand from the king. Who could have blamed him for taking the comfort of good food and drink after having nothing but the Israelite version of MREs and canteen water? His honor and integrity even extended to denying himself the opportunity of sleeping with his wife, Bathsheba, whose beauty had caught David's eye. Consider how many of his fellow soldiers would have thought less of Uriah if he had taken comfort at home. Unless men, even men of God, are far different today than they were then, I would guess that very few would have criticized him. It is more likely that they would have thought he was crazy for missing the opportunity.

Uriah's commitment to God and the men he was responsible for was stronger than the fear of being mocked or thought crazy. His commitment was stronger than his natural desires for good chow and the marriage bed. If a Marine leader has even a portion of this type of commitment to God and those he or she serves, that leader can be depended on to do the right and best thing regardless of the circumstances.

It's obvious that Uriah wasn't a man who was easily pressured into doing anything. He demonstrated a very real moral courage when he told his sovereign that he would not enjoy the comforts of home. David's reputation must have been above reproach to those he led. He was a warrior who had defeated Goliath[1] and killed "his tens of thousands."[2] But Uriah had no trouble telling David what he would not do. That type of fortitude only wells up from a deep conviction that serving God takes precedent over obeying any man regardless of his position or fame. Uriah also had the physical courage to desire returning to battle when he probably could have milked his stay in Jerusalem quite a while, considering that he was definitely in the king's favor at this time.

This analysis of Uriah is based on a relatively short record of his life, but the facts bear out the conclusions reached. It is also an important point to consider, that Uriah's strength was not limited to one of the three core values of Marines. He demonstrated strength in each. He did not demonstrate one aspect of these values at the expense of another. His honor and commitment and courage were intertwined in his character. Uriah, as we see in this vignette, was the complete package we should all aspire to as people of God and Marines. It is interesting to note that the Marine Corps had been in existence for more than 200 years before courage, honor, and commitment were codified as core values. Having a set of values that everyone is expected to live up to is appropriate for an organization that is given the awesome respon-

---

[1] 1 Samuel 17

[2] 1 Samuel 18:6-8

sibility of defending the nation. They are meant to be more than a slogan. Courage, honor, and commitment are intended to become deeply held beliefs from which an individual's actions, like Uriah's, flow.

CHAPTER 2

Semper Fidelis and the Greatest Commandment

I f you look for the reason why Marines act the way we do, why we hold so firmly to the honor of our traditions, you'll find that our motto, "Semper Fidelis," sums it up. The Corps is an institution that America can rely on to do its duty. Each Marine is an individual upon whom America can rely to do his or her duty. When courage wanes or when personal desires begin to overtake the higher purpose, "Always Faithful" remains the foundation of a Marine. Individuals may go astray, they may even rebel, but Semper Fidelis is the standard to which we all are held. To be always faithful presumes that there is something worthy of our faith. Faithfulness to a corrupt system or leader is empty of all honor. The unswerving dedication of the Nazis to Adolph Hitler wins them no respect in history; quite the opposite in fact. In America, our solemn oath is sworn, not to individuals or organizations, but to the Constitution and the authority that flows from it. If you strip away all the public laws and regulations, all the principles and traits, and all the traditions, Semper Fidelis is the greatest commandment of the Corps. Hopefully, you already have an idea where this is headed.

> Hearing that Jesus had silenced the Sadducees, the Pharisees got together. One of them, an expert in the law, tested him with this question: "Teacher, which is the greatest commandment in the Law?" Jesus replied: "'Love the Lord your God with all your heart and with all your soul and with all your mind.' This is the first and greatest commandment."
> Matthew 22:34-38

In the same way that Semper Fidelis is the foundation for the conduct of the Corps and the individual Marine, "Love the Lord your God with all your heart and with all your soul and with all your mind" is the foundation for your conduct and motivation as a man or woman of God. The motto and the greatest commandment can certainly be used as touchstones in times of fear or temptation to remind us of our duty. But they aren't just tools that hang on your belt to use when the time is right. These are truths that must be at the core of who you are. These must be the truths from which all your actions well up and flow out. If these are not, you may come to the realization that you are just going through the motions and not living up to your potential as a Marine nor, more importantly, living the abundant life that Jesus has promised us as His people.

Dependability: the certainty of proper performance of duty.

For Christians, dependability is a reflection in our lives of the One who is truly constant. A Christian should remain constant, acknowledging faith in the order in which God has set His kingdom.

> But select capable men from all the people—men who fear God, trustworthy men who hate dishonest gain—and appoint them as officials over thousands, hundreds, fifties and tens.
>
> Exodus 18:21

> And the things you have heard me say in the presence of many witnesses entrust to reliable men who will also be qualified to teach others.
>
> 2 Timothy 2:2

> "Well done, my good servant!" his master replied. "Because you have been trustworthy in a very small matter, take charge of ten cities."
>
> Luke 19:17

Integrity: uprightness of character and soundness of moral principles includes the qualities of truthfulness and honesty.

Of all the leadership traits, integrity is the one most closely linked with our spiritual selves. In an age of near absolute relativism, the ideas of upright character and sound moral principles seem somewhat quaint. Our current legal climate demonstrates the modern view whereby taking responsibility for one's actions is neither expected nor encouraged.

The man of integrity walks securely, but he who takes crooked paths will be found out.

Proverbs 10:9

My lips will not speak wickedness, and my tongue will utter no deceit. I will never admit you are in the right; till I die, I will not deny my integrity. I will maintain my righteousness and never let go of it; my conscience will not reproach me as long as I live.

Job 27:4-6

O LORD our God, as for all this abundance that we have provided for building you a temple for your holy name, it comes from your hand, and all of it belongs to you. I know, my God, that you test the heart and are pleased with integrity. All these things have I given willingly and with honest intent. And now I have seen with joy how willingly your people who are here have given to you. O LORD, God of our fathers Abraham, Isaac, and Israel, keep this desire in the hearts of your people forever, and keep their hearts loyal to you.

1 Chronicles 29:16-18

Dear friends, I urge you, as aliens and strangers in the world, to abstain from sinful desires, which war against your soul. Live such good lives among the pagans that, though they accuse you of doing wrong, they may see your good deeds and glorify God on the day He visits us.

1 Peter 2:12

CHAPTER 3

Who Better to Carry Out the Great Commission?

⸺ ⧢ ⸺

Then Jesus came to them and said, "All authority in heaven and on earth has been given to me. Therefore go and make disciples of all nations, baptizing them in the name of the Father and of the Son and of the Holy Spirit, and teaching them to obey everything I have commanded you. And surely I am with you always, to the very end of the age."

Matthew 28:17-21

Jesus' words from the Great Commission will have a familiar ring to anyone who has served in the Armed Forces. They are the words of a true commander. He establishes His authority, identifies the mission and tasks to be completed, and provides personal encouragement to His troops. Stop for a moment and consider what He is telling His apostles.

Leave the comfort of home and dedicate yourself to a difficult mission in an uncertain environment for a greater purpose than your own welfare. A member of the armed forces will also recognize what Jesus is saying because he or she has done exactly that in their own life.

"Authority"

Before an American puts on a uniform or picks up a rifle he must know under what authority he is operating. He must acknowledge by solemn oath that he recognizes the authority of the Constitution, the president, and those appointed over him. In addition to confirming the loyalty of the individual, this oath should remove any doubts he has about what he's getting into. He's not just joining a local club or fraternity. In the same way, Jesus explained to His disciples that the Father gave Him the authority to direct their efforts.

"Therefore Go"

One sure thing about joining the military—you will travel. The Navy promises that you will see the world if you join. The other implication to going is leaving what is known and comfortable. There is an element of self-sacrifice to the simple verb *go*. We're not told specifically where we will be going every time. Neither Jesus nor the Marine Corps will make any promises about what you will find when you get there. There's a lot of the world that's best left unseen. One of the interesting parts about moving around is that you get to see the diversity in the body of Christ.[3] My family went from a suburban Washington, D.C., congregation with six elders, a full-time preacher, and a youth minister to a congregation in Okinawa with no leadership or preacher. I found myself, to my great shock, delivering sermons and occasionally leading singing. Since my denomination sings without instrumental accompaniment, you can't imagine how scary that was for both me and the congregation. Those smaller military congregations were also the most racially diverse we ever attended; it was wonderful because of the different styles of worship. It has been incredibly moving to hear *Amazing Grace* sung simultaneously in Japanese and English; we really began to see what Paul meant when he said, "There is neither Jew nor Greek, slave nor free, male nor female, for you are all one in Christ Jesus."[4] But we went through some hard times, too, with bitter and immature quarrels over doctrine and traditions. We had no chance to do anything but grow in the faith crucible of small remote churches. You will also come into contact with locals through the church who you wouldn't have known otherwise. Life and opportunities to learn and grow really opened up for my family when we got to know native Hawaiians and Okinawans at church.

"Make disciples"

Jesus' direction here isn't halfhearted. *Make* is a strong word and it brings a heavy responsibility. A

---

[3] 1 Corinthians 12:27
Now you are the body of Christ, and each one of you is a part of it.
[4] Galatians 3:28

disciple is an apprentice, one who dedicates herself to not just a teacher, but to a way of life. To make someone a disciple requires the maker to dedicate themselves to that disciple as well. If we stop and think about it, making disciples is the most natural thing in the world for Marines. We who wear or have worn the uniform were certainly made disciples in the Marine Corps way of life. After Officer Candidate School or recruit training, the instruction and cultural immersion in every aspect of our lives continues until the day we hang up the boots. We have endless formations, classes, techniques of military instruction, school circles, and officers' calls that are all designed to bring us into an increasingly common understanding of our chosen profession. Master gunnys attend some of the same instructional gatherings that lance corporals attend and the informal discipling in the form of counseling, squaring someone away, or just taking a newbie under your wing occurs even more frequently. Shouldn't that same attitude apply to being a Christian and making disciples? Maybe it's harder because no matter how long we have been a Christian we all feel a little like "newbs," considering the awesome and eternal family we've joined. But that should make our efforts to grow in maturity and disciple younger Christians all the more urgent. We are perfectly suited for the job.

"Obey"

Not a popular word or concept in today's individualistic society. The military is one of the last bastions of obedience. It must be so. Close order drill is designed primarily to demonstrate the value of instant obedience to orders by members of group. The idea being, of course, that in combat instant obedience will overcome natural fear to get the mission accomplished and will save lives. To obey assumes that the commands and desires of the leader are communicated well. In close order drill the unit leader doesn't make up personal commands but uses the language of the drill manual. I noted an exception to this rule during my time at OCS in the summer of 1983. Candidate Roddy was being tested in his ability to drill a platoon. We formed up well and Roddy issued his first command—except that Roddy forgot the pause between the preparatory command and the execution command. "Right (pause) Face!" came out "Right Face (pause)." And the pause grew as it dawned on Roddy that he'd messed up. Instead of folding his hand, he forged ahead and yelled in a high-pitched voice "March!" Thus, "Right Face, March" was added to posterity. The result was not all snap and pop, half of us turned, half didn't, and most of us, including the evaluator, burst out laughing.

Obedience also requires establishing a bond of trust. If a leader's orders can result in the death of those under his charge, those being led have to trust their leader and devote themselves to following. Their obedience, even in the face of great danger, proves their devotion either to the leader or to the institution that leader represents. In my days in the Corps, I was led by a few jerks and even by a couple of incompetents. The good news for Christians is that the leader we are called to obey is perfect. He created the world and keeps it turning. Our goal in close order drill is simple efficiency. The goal of Christian obedience goes infinitely beyond efficiency and gets to the heart of who God is and why we were created. Jesus tells us, "If anyone loves me, he will obey my teaching. My Father will *love* him, and we will come to him and make our home with him."[5] Rather than forcing obedience from the top down, Almighty God reveals Himself and demonstrates His love, which draws us to Him in loving obedience. We can completely trust Christ and our Father in the face of the gravest danger or daily hassles to know what is right for us and to have our best interests at heart.

As I considered the Great Commission in this light, I was reminded of the letter U. S. Marine Major General James Mattis wrote to the Marines and sailors of the First Marine Division on the eve of the invasion of Iraq in March 2003. In his letter he said:

> *For decades, Saddam Hussein has tortured, imprisoned, raped and murdered the Iraqi people; invaded neighboring countries without provocation; and threatened the world with weapons of mass destruction. The time has come to end his reign of terror. On your young shoulders rest the hopes of mankind.*
>
> *When I give you the word, together we will cross the Line of Departure, close with those forces that choose to fight, and destroy them.*

---

[5] John 14:23

Our fight is not with the Iraqi people, nor is it with members of the Iraqi army who choose to surrender. While we will move swiftly and aggressively against those who resist, we will treat all others with decency, demonstrating chivalry and soldierly compassion for people who have endured a lifetime under Saddam's oppression. Chemical attacks, treachery, and the use of the innocent as human shields can be expected, as can unethical tactics. Take it all in stride. Be the hunter, not the hunted: never allow your unit to be caught with its guard down. Use good judgment and act in the best interest of our Nation. You are part of the world's most feared and trusted force. Engage your brain before you engage your weapon. Share your courage with each other as we enter the uncertain terrain north of the Line of Departure. Keep faith with your comrades on your left and right and Marine Air overhead. Fight with a happy heart and strong spirit.

For the mission's sake, our country's sake, and the sake of the men who carried the Division's colors in past battles—who fought for life and never lost their nerve—carry out your mission and keep your honor clean. Demonstrate to the world that there is 'No Better Friend, No Worse Enemy' than a U. S. Marine.

Mattis establishes his authority for ordering the attack through his signature and title. He sets the stage with the higher purpose his force is called to and then encourages them to carry out their task to the best of their ability. He also lets them know that he will be with them: "Together we will cross the Line of Departure." I'm not trying to compare General Mattis to Jesus Christ, but this is a good point of reference as we begin to consider the parallels of lives committed to serving our nation and serving our Savior.

Tact: the ability to deal with others without creating offense.

Tact is a natural outgrowth of respect for others and humility about ourselves in relation to others. Other Christians have the same standing before the throne of God we do. We should extend the courtesy of our words to non-Christians because we share the same fallen heritage with them and are redeemed only through God's grace.

> Let your conversation be always full of grace, seasoned with salt, so that you may know how to answer everyone.
>
> Colossians 4:6

> The proud and arrogant man—'Mocker' is his name—behaves with overweening pride.
>
> Proverbs 21:24

> For by the grace given me I say to every one of you: Do not think of yourself more highly than you ought, but rather think of yourself

with sober judgment, in accordance with the measure of faith God has given you.

Romans 12:3

Instead, speaking the truth in love, we will in all things grow up into him who is the Head, that is, Christ.

Ephesians 4:15

Live in harmony with one another. Do not be proud, but be willing to associate with people of low position. Do not be conceited.

Romans 12:16

Do nothing out of selfish ambition or vain conceit, but in humility consider others better than yourselves.

Philippians 2:3

This is also why you pay taxes, for the authorities are God's servants, who give their full time to governing. Give everyone what you owe him: If you owe taxes, pay taxes; if revenue, then revenue; if respect, then respect; if honor, then honor.

Romans 13:7

Enthusiasm: the display of sincere interest and exuberance in the performance of duty.

To be too enthusiastic about things today is to risk being made fun of. In our society a certain world-weary cynicism is expected even among teenagers who haven't experienced anything of the world to be weary about. But when the daily grind begins to wear us down, we have the higher purposes of God and Corps to keep us from burning out. But the basis for our enthusiasm is not solely conceptual; we are offered countless opportunities in ever-changing circumstances for true enthusiasm about the work God has put before us. Our enthusiasm also encourages those around us. Neither God nor the Marine Corps is looking for empty-headed cheerleading; there are too many good reasons to be sincerely enthusiastic about being a Christian and being a Marine.

Never be lacking in zeal, but keep your spiritual fervor, serving the Lord.

Romans 12:11

For I know your eagerness to help, and I have been boasting about it to the Macedonians, telling them that since last year you in Achaia were ready to give; and your enthusiasm has stirred most of them to action.

2 Corinthians 9:2

In addition, we are sending with them our brother who has often proved to us in many ways that he is zealous, and now even more so because of his great confidence in you.

2 Corinthians 8:22

For Titus not only welcomed our appeal, but he is coming to you with much enthusiasm and on his own initiative.

2 Corinthians 8:17

It is not good to have zeal without knowledge, nor to be hasty and miss the way.

Proverbs 19:2

It is fine to be zealous, provided the purpose is good, and to be so always and not just when I am with you.

Galatians 4:18

Loyalty: the quality of faithfulness to country, the Corps, the unit, to one's seniors, subordinates and peers.

Membership in the Corps means that your personal motto becomes Always Faithful. Membership in Christ's body means the same thing, but our loyalty is to Jesus above all else. Our faithfulness to the Corps may require us to speak in opposition to commanders' policies when those policies are put in place solely for the benefit or advancement of the commander. Opposition of this type may be condemned as disloyalty, but that argument is invalid because our higher responsibility is always loyalty to the Corps and what it stands for, rather than to an individual. Our loyalty to Christ will never be put to the test in that manner because God has given all authority to Him and His motives are always true and perfect. There is no room for gray areas or variable levels of loyalty to Christ because of the changing circumstances in which we find ourselves. The greatest commandment removes all doubt. "Love the Lord your God with all your heart and with all your soul and with all your mind," leaves little room for rationalization or loyalties elsewhere. Those three "alls" are definitive. Biblical examples of loyalty and faithfulness are wonderful to read. The stories of Ruth's loyalty to Naomi in hard times and David's loyalty to Saul, even when Saul didn't deserve David's loyalty, are truly inspiring.

> Uriah said to David, "The ark and Israel and Judah are staying in tents, and my master Joab and my lord's men are camped in the open fields. How could I go to my house to eat and drink and lie with my wife? As surely as you live, I will not do such a thing!"
>
> 2 Samuel 11:11

> Each one should use whatever gift he has received to serve others, faithfully administering God's grace in its various forms.
>
> 1 Peter 4:10

> His master replied, "Well done, good and faithful servant! You have been faithful with a few things; I will put you in charge of many things. Come and share your master's happiness!"
>
> Matthew 25:21

But the fruit of the Spirit is love, joy, peace, patience, kindness, goodness, *faithfulness*, gentleness, and self-control.

Galatians 5:22

He holds victory in store for the upright, he is a shield to those whose walk is blameless, for he guards the course of the just and protects the way of his faithful ones.

Proverbs 2:7-8

Love and faithfulness keep a king safe; through love his throne is made secure.

Proverbs 20:28

CHAPTER 4

Can a Marine Really Be a Christian and Vice Versa?

———— ⌘ ————

We need to be sure in our hearts that what we have chosen to do for a living does not bring us personally into conflict with Him whom we have chosen to follow. Having this matter settled is especially important for people who have chosen to be Marines, since the Corps becomes so much a part of who we are. Is having a secular career in the military a roadblock to your spiritual life? The answer is yes—if that secular career, just like banking or sales, takes precedence over your obedience to God. A minister whose actions and heart are not turned toward God is less acceptable to God than a used car salesman who seeks to be Christ-like in what he does at work. But what about military service specifically? Given the loving nature of the Christian way, wouldn't it be reasonable for Jesus to exclude soldiers? Or, since Jesus' sacrifice is for all, wouldn't it be reasonable to see Him only grudgingly permit military people to be saved, perhaps at a distance? Jesus apparently did not exclude military men from His kingdom; this is demonstrated in His actions when He healed the Roman centurion's servant in Capernaum.

When Jesus had entered Capernaum, a centurion came to him, asking for help. "Lord," he said, "my servant lies at home paralyzed and in terrible suffering."

Jesus said to him, "I will go and heal him."

The centurion replied, "Lord, I do not deserve to have you come under my roof. But just say the word, and my servant will be healed. For I myself am a man under authority, with soldiers under me. I tell this one, 'Go,' and he goes; and that one, 'Come,' and he comes. I say to my servant, 'Do this,' and he does it."

When Jesus heard this, he was astonished and said to those following him, "I tell you the truth, I have not found anyone in Israel with such great faith. I say to you that many will come from the east and the west, and will take their places at the feast with Abraham, Isaac and Jacob in the kingdom of heaven. But the subjects of the kingdom will be thrown outside, into the darkness, where there will be weeping and gnashing of teeth."

Then Jesus said to the centurion, "Go! It
will be done just as you believed it would."
And his servant was healed at that very hour.
Matthew 8:5-13

Christ goes much further in including soldiers in
His kingdom. When the kingdom was opened to the
Gentiles, it was another centurion, Cornelius, who
was chosen to receive this monumental blessing of
God. The story is told in Acts 10. A close look shows
that God worked through Cornelius first, to call Peter
to Cornelius' home. Peter learned that day, "How true
it is that God does not show favoritism but accepts
men from every nation who fear him and do what
is right." There's no evidence that either the centurion at Capernaum or Cornelius gave up his military
position because of his new-found faith in Christ.
There's no evidence that any soldier was expected
to abandon military life to be a Christian. The key to
serving God as a Marine today is no different than it
was for great warriors like David and Joshua: serve
Him first and fully.

So what about the flip side of the question?
Marines are not excluded from the kingdom, but does
the Corps exclude Christians? Are the values of the
gentle King at odds with service as a Marine? Is there
anything we find in Christianity that makes it incom-
patible with serving in the military? While others may
oppose Christianity or the exercise of our faith, our
rights are firmly established in law and regulation.
The First Amendment to the U. S. Constitution guar-
antees the free exercise of religion and that doesn't

change when you put on a uniform. Commanders are charged with the responsibility to provide for the free exercise of faith by those under their command. The office of military chaplain was created specifically to assist commanders in the discharge of this responsibility.[6]

Marine Corps Order 1730.6D states that Command Religious Programs, "will provide opportunities for participants to express and nurture their religious faith." Official policy makes it clear that our faith is to be honored. Religious faith is a cornerstone of building Marines. Marine Corps Reference Publication 6-11B, the *Users' Guide for Discussion about Marine Corps Values* states:

> Part of belonging to the Marine team and family involves incorporating the values of that team into the daily lives of each of its members. We all understand, and must subscribe to, our Corps values: honor, courage, and commitment. There are other values which we honor as defenders of the Constitution: the ideals of democracy, fairness, *faith*, and freedom. These values, and the basic concept of right and wrong, are cornerstones in building Marines. These basic values are the "anchor points" of many of the lessons contained in this guidebook.

---

[6] DoD Directive 1304.19, "Appointment of Chaplains for the Military Services"

Justice: giving reward and punishment according to merits of the case in question. The ability to administer a system of rewards and punishments impartially and consistently.

Marine leaders are expected to be firm but fair in their dealings with subordinates. In a brotherhood that prides itself on egalitarian principles and the commonality of mutual respect between its members, one of the surest ways to lose the respect of Marines is to demonstrate favoritism or vindictiveness toward an individual. Exercising impartiality is particularly important in the case of officers who have the authority to administer non-judicial punishment. The effects of an unjust decision in NJP can limit a Marine's growth or end a career prematurely. Human decisions will reflect human frailty in judgment, but impartiality and consistency are cornerstones of military life and the Christian walk. You also have every right to be treated justly as a Christian in the military.

> If you really keep the royal law found in Scripture, "Love your neighbor as yourself," you are doing right. But if you show favoritism, you sin and are convicted by the law as lawbreakers.
>
> James 2:8-9

> And the word of the LORD came again to Zechariah: "This is what the LORD Almighty says: 'Administer true justice; show mercy and compassion to one another'"
>
> Zechariah 7:8

Do not follow the crowd in doing wrong. When you give testimony in a lawsuit, do not pervert justice by siding with the crowd.

Exodus 23:2

Do not pervert justice; do not show partiality to the poor or favoritism to the great, but judge your neighbor fairly.

Leviticus 19:15

Righteousness and justice are the foundation of your throne; love and faithfulness go before you.

Psalm 89:14

He has showed you, O man, what is good. And what does the LORD require of you? To act justly and to love mercy and to walk humbly with your God.

Micah 6:8

CHAPTER 5

Pure Religion in the Barracks

———— ⌇ ————

Having the freedom to exercise your faith doesn't mean that everyone around you will accept or even respect your beliefs. The Marine Corps is made up of a diverse population that reflects to some extent the diversity found in the American population. Be prepared to lead Marines with Christian faith that matches or exceeds your own. Be prepared to work with Marines who are devoted to a set of beliefs completely foreign to you. Be prepared for Marines who have never considered any belief system other than the one they learned in the Corps. We have to respect the beliefs with which we disagree because we must respect God's decision to give people the ability to decide for themselves whether they accept or reject Him. In today's culture we are expected to respect and even celebrate the differences and beliefs of others. Celebrating those differences that we know cause others to reject Christ is a bridge too far. Respect does not extend to agreeing with a godless or other-god position, nor should respect cause us to consider thinking that those other beliefs are equal in value to a belief in Jesus Christ. Elevating any idea to equal value with the truth is to deny that truth exists. It is sometimes difficult to hold to the truth because it can seem so unfair to others. Diversity and tolerance have become the cornerstones of the new secular religion in the Western world; they are a great disguise for the lies that keep people in ignorance, because they seem so fair. Real fairness, real equity, doesn't elevate us all to god-like status. Equity has to be based in the truth and truth isn't relative; it is no different for you than it is for me. Truth doesn't depend on our perspective or our experiences in life. That is a bold statement, but Jesus had an even bolder statement: "I am the way and the truth and the life. No one comes to the Father except through me."[7]

In addition to spiritual relativism, the world wants us to accept a moral relativism. There is no universal truth, so there can be no universal right or wrong. To keep things on a practical rather than philosophical level, we can always rely on the book of James to guide us. James has something simple to say about our religion and the moral standards we find in the world. He says, "Religion that God our Father accepts as pure and faultless is this: to look after orphans and widows in their distress and to keep oneself from being polluted by the world." We'll look at helping

---

[7] John 14:6

46

others in distress in a later chapter; for now let's look at personal pollution. Life in the barracks can be a real test of character. Profane and extreme behavior that seems to define today's American culture washes over us from all sides. What was once stereotypical of a hard-drinking and rough Marine is now common behavior in all walks of life. Pornography, cruel humor, and a studied nonchalance toward offensive things is a part of daily life for young people today. It is difficult to keep from being polluted when corruption laps around your ankles at the best of times and rises like a tidal wave with regularity. It seems that the best defense against being polluted is an offensive mindset. Proactively helping someone who needs you turns the mind in a Christ-like direction and keeps faith from becoming just a way to manage the sin in your life. While you may not find many widows and orphans in the squad bay, you will certainly find plenty of folks in distress.

The other element of defense against pollution is the truth. When lies and profanity flow around you, fall back on what you know is true. Even if you don't confront the profane or the liar openly, don't dismiss them easily. Don't give the pollution the benefit of the doubt. If you don't acknowledge, at least in your thoughts, what is true and good, you'll find that you become worn down and desensitized to evil. We need to be sensitive and clear headed, because we are called to be the search and rescue crew of God, not passengers on the party boat. At my age, I don't have much energy for or interest in wild living, but there is plenty of pollution even for a guy like me. I grew up in the 1960's and was raised by the television. Andy Griffith and Dick Van Dyke have been replaced by Ozzy and Sharon. But you don't have to be intentionally watching a freak show on MTV to get covered in the slime. The message of the day seems to be sex and contempt for everyone but yourself. The best example of a pollution-free attitude in action comes where Joseph is stalked by Potiphar's wife in Genesis 39:2-12.

The LORD was with Joseph and he prospered, and he lived in the house of his Egyptian master. When his master saw that the LORD was with him and that the LORD gave him success in everything he did, Joseph found favor in his eyes and became his attendant. Potiphar put him in charge of his household, and he entrusted to his care everything he owned. From the time he put him in charge of his household and of all that he owned, the LORD blessed the household of the Egyptian because of Joseph. The blessing of the LORD was on everything Potiphar had, both in the house and in the field. So he left in Joseph's care everything he had; with Joseph in charge, he did not concern himself with anything except the food he ate.

Now Joseph was well-built and handsome, and after a while his master's wife took notice of Joseph and said, "Come to bed with me!"

But he refused. "With me in charge," he told her, "my master does not concern himself with anything in the house; everything he owns he has entrusted to my care. No one is greater in this house than I am. My master has withheld nothing from me except you, because you are his wife. How then could I do such a wicked thing and sin against God?" And though she spoke to Joseph day after day, he refused to go to bed with her or even be with her.

One day he went into the house to attend to his duties, and none of the household servants was inside. She caught him by his cloak and said, "Come to bed with me!" But he left his cloak in her hand and ran out of the house.

Even as a young man, Joseph was able to see through the "good deal" of her offer of easy sex to the truth of the situation. Giving in would have been a betrayal of Potiphar, but more importantly, it would have dishonored God who had provided Joseph with such abundance. The Lord has provided us with an even greater abundance by redeeming us completely from the corruption of the world and offering us a joyful and productive life, rather than a life spent chasing short-lived gratification. We need to have the Christian honor that causes us to run from crude behavior, pornography, and alcohol—even when things temporarily turn out wrong as it did later for Joseph in Genesis 39.

She kept his cloak beside her until his master came home. Then she told him this story: "That Hebrew slave you brought us came to me to make sport of me. But as soon as I screamed for help, he left his cloak beside me and ran out of the house."

When his master heard the story his wife told him, saying, "This is how your slave treated me," he burned with anger. Joseph's master took him and put him in prison, the place where the king's prisoners were confined.

But while Joseph was there in the prison, the LORD was with him; he showed him kindness and granted him favor in the eyes of the prison warden.

vv. 16-21

From a worldly point of view, behaving in a way that honors God doesn't always end happily as it did for Joseph. But from a God's eye view, honoring Him brings peace and joy that the world knows nothing about. In keeping himself from being polluted, Joseph proved himself reliable, ready for the larger task of sustaining Israel for which God had chosen him.

The pollution doesn't have to be blatant like most music videos or the morally reprehensible humor you see on so many of today's cleverly animated shows. Pollution can be anything that takes our focus from God and begins to affect that relationship with Him. I read a lot of novels and when I get wrapped up in the story I lose track of time and what I should be doing. I also find that I will overlook steamy sex scenes and horrible graphic violence if the story is good. Although reading seems a relatively harmless activity and is in most cases, it is easy for me to find myself desensitized and wallowing mentally in someone else's fantasy world.

Bearing: creating a favorable impression in carriage, appearance, and personal conduct at all times.

The two complementary parts of bearing are to know who you are and to whom you belong and then to carry yourself in an appropriate manner. While Marines expect each other to carry themselves like Marines, don't be too quick to be impressed by physical appearance, a score of 300 points on the physical fitness test, or a commanding voice. Those attributes certainly score in the positive column, but may mask flaws in character or ability. As we see in 1 Samuel 9, Israel thought Saul was exactly who they were looking for in a king. Although he had the strong and handsome appearance of a king, he lacked the character necessary to handle the responsibility. Keep in mind the words of the prophet Isaiah as he describes Jesus, the King of kings: "He grew up before him like a tender shoot, and like a root out of dry ground. He had no beauty or majesty to attract us to him, nothing in his appearance that we should desire him."[8] Our Christian bearing should well up from a heart committed to Christ and the things of

---

[8] Isaiah 53:2

God. There should be enough evidence in the way we act to convict us of belonging to Jesus.

> But you are a chosen people, a royal priest-hood, a holy nation, a people belonging to God, that you may declare the praises of him who called you out of darkness into his wonderful light.
>
> 1 Peter 2:9

> Similarly, encourage the young men to be self-controlled. In everything set them an example by doing what is good. In your teaching show integrity, seriousness and soundness of speech that cannot be condemned, so that those who oppose you may be ashamed because they have nothing bad to say about us.
>
> Titus 2:6-8

> Nor should there be obscenity, foolish talk or coarse joking, which are out of place, but rather thanksgiving.
>
> Ephesians 5:4

> I will set before my eyes no vile thing.
>
> Psalm 101:3

Courage: the mental quality that recognizes fear of danger or criticism, but enables a man to proceed in the face of it with calmness and firmness.

It is undeniable that Christians are called to be humble and loving. These are certainly characteristics of our Savior and the great men of God throughout history. Those outside the kingdom looking in can mistake the gentleness of God's people for a lack of manliness or inner strength. Jesus, however, epitomizes the Marine Corps definition of courage. He continually defied those in worldly authority when they were wrong, knowing that His defiance would lead to a cruel death. Consider the anguish He experienced in the Garden before His crucifixion and the courageous manner in which he went forward in the face of the personal horror He knew was to come.

If you spend time in the halls of a headquarters building, you will find photographs of Marines who have won the Medal of Honor in past wars. It is easy to see that our nation honors its fighting men who have taken action in the face of great personal danger. For God's people, courage is more often expressed by unhesitatingly placing ourselves in the Lord's hands when something inside is screaming for us to take action for ourselves. We place ourselves in God's hands, knowing that He is in control and is able, regardless of the situation. When all evidence points to a bad outcome heading our way, our faith gives us strength to stand strong and not be afraid. Shadrach, Meshach, and Abednego demonstrated an abundance of godly courage when they refused to worship Nebuchadnezzar's idol.

> "But if you do not worship it, you will be thrown immediately into a blazing furnace. Then what god will be able to rescue you from my hand?" Shadrach, Meshach and Abednego

replied to the king, "O Nebuchadnezzar, we do not need to defend ourselves before you in this matter. If we are thrown into the blazing furnace, the God we serve is able to save us from it, and he will rescue us from your hand, O king. *But even if he does not, we want you to know,* O king, that we will not serve your gods or worship the image of gold you have set up.

Daniel 3:15-18

Be strong and courageous. Do not be afraid or terrified because of them, for the Lord your God goes with you; he will never leave you nor forsake you.

Deuteronomy 31:6

Do not be afraid of those who kill the body but cannot kill the soul. Rather, be afraid of the One who can destroy both soul and body in hell.

Matthew 10:28

Be on your guard; stand firm in the faith; be men of courage; be strong. Do everything in love.

1 Corinthians 16:13-14

CHAPTER 6

Idolatry in the Ranks

———❈———

There is nothing wrong with taking satisfaction in our work or career. According to Solomon, satisfaction with our work is a gift from God. He said, "Then I realized that it is good and proper for a man to eat and drink, and to find satisfaction in his toilsome labor under the sun during the few days of life God has given him—for this is his lot. Moreover, when God gives any man wealth and possessions, and enables him to enjoy them, to accept his lot and be happy in his work—this is a gift of God."[9]

Not every job is equally honorable. Serving a greater good should provide a greater satisfaction. We believe that there is no higher place of honor in the American armed forces than the place occupied by our Marine Corps. If you ask recruits why they joined the Marines, more often than not their answer will revolve

---

[9] Ecclesiastes 5:18

around the idea that they wanted to be part of the best. That idea lasts for a lifetime in most cases.

Most of the Marines I've known over the past twenty-five years were deeply changed by their service. I retired a couple of years ago and now work with about thirty-five other retired and former Marines at a defense contractor facility near Quantico. On 10 November every year we read General Lejeune's message and cut the birthday cake, recognizing the oldest and youngest former Marines present. That short ceremony, marking the birth of the Marine Corps, is the most well attended event of the many we put on throughout the year. The bond that still exists between those who have served as Marines always impresses the other 130 or so civilians who come to watch. The Marine Corps gives many of us something much better in our lives than what we had before we joined. Men and women searching for a calling to something higher than themselves can take great pride in their position as a Marine.

There is also a redemptive quality to serving in the Corps. Mine may be an extreme case, but I doubt it. I was only twenty-one but was well on my way to becoming an alcoholic. I was working in the Norfolk Naval Shipyard as pipe fitter in the sewage gang. My workplace was the dry dock where the raw sewage ran overboard from the ships and onto the dry dock floor. A significant part of my day was spent washing sewage into drains with a fire hose. It wasn't really as glamorous as it sounds! You can imagine that even a little bit of the pride and self-esteem I picked up at boot camp went a long way after working in the shipyard. In fact, I joined the Marine Corps because of the great contrast I saw between the men in the Corps and myself. In those days Marines guarded the gates to the navy bases and often stood post, dressed in modified blues. In my mind they always stood out as much sharper and more vibrant than everything else that surrounded them. One day I was sitting in a truck on a pier by the *U.S.S. Independence* when three Marines from the ship's Marine detachment came down the brow. In the middle of all of the industrial grime of the shipyard and the general slovenliness of the sailors, these guys were awesome. They wore bright white skivvy shirts tucked into sharply creased sateen utility trousers and spit-shined boots. The fact that they stood out is particularly ironic because the task they were coming down the brow to perform was none other than emptying a large garbage can. Their appearance wasn't what kept my attention; it was the fact that they dumped the garbage with a military precision. They turned it into a little game of "present can" and "ready... dump!" They were at the bottom of the organization doing a menial task (I knew something about that!), but were doing it with dignity, and doing it on their own smart-alecky terms.

My wife will certainly confirm that I was redeemed from a miserable life when I shipped out to Parris Island. But we know that the Marine Corps cannot save anyone from eternal destruction. Solomon confirms throughout the book of Ecclesiastes that faithful and honorable service to anything but God is meaningless. A stellar thirty-year career will amount to absolutely nothing on the

Day of Judgment. If you stick around the Corps long enough you will meet individuals who have no identity other than that of a Marine. It consumes them, body and soul, even to the exclusion of having an identity within their families or communities. The uniform, the rank, and their professional competence all confirm their worth. The train wreck for these individuals comes at discharge or retirement when the Marine identity can no longer be the center of who they are. No matter how worthwhile the work, we all have to resist being consumed by what we do for a living.

It's ironic that my real redemption by Christ came about ten years after enlisting, when I had come a long way from the bottom of the dry dock. I was a captain with two tours in the fleet under my belt and had been selected to attend the Amphibious Warfare School, which was a pretty big deal in those days. I had also been asked for by name to be on the Marine Air Ground Task Force Instruction Team at Quantico with General Van Riper. My career was looking promising and my family life was wonderful. I knew that I was lucky or fortunate, but felt an emptiness like something was missing, like I wasn't complete. After working so hard by my own power for years to build a life, I realized how much I needed to be saved from the life I had built because it was built on skewed perspectives and contained more than a few idols. Those idols had to go.

I also had to get rid of the feeling that being a Marine somehow added to my spiritual status. That idea may sound ridiculous, but that is how I felt before I became a Christian. Maybe that line in the hymn that talks about heaven's streets being guarded by United States Marines had something to do with it. After all, I was a lot better person than I had been before I left for Parris Island. I felt respectable, and that was a new feeling for me. All things being equal, I felt I should get some credit for serving and exercising all that new-found self-discipline. All things, of course, are not equal—what counts is our trust in Christ. We cannot save ourselves by effort or membership, no matter how exclusive the club.

Pride in achievement and tradition is wonderful but arrogance is born from self-satisfaction in belonging to the right group. The Pharisees thought that their lineage as Abraham's sons, their position in the synagogue, and their strict adherence to the traditions of their fathers advanced them spiritually. But Jesus had hard words for them and singled them out as examples of hypocrisy. The pride they had in their traditional relationship with God blinded them to the fact that God was standing before them with a new message. The Pharisees were extraordinarily faithful, but their focus became faithfulness to tradition rather than faithfulness to God. If pride and achievement in a religious body wasn't enough to win the approval of Christ for the Pharisees, pride in a secular organization like the Marine Corps, no matter how honorable, certainly will take us no farther.

Judgment: the ability to weigh facts and possible solutions on which to base sound decisions.

Good judgment in human terms comes from experience; often it comes as a result of learning from our mistakes. Judgment intersects with wisdom in the realm of common sense or discernment. But it has not been my experience that gaining wisdom follows a distinct pattern. It is not clear that gaining wisdom or developing good judgment is a sure thing for all of us. One of the mottos of my Basic School class was, "common sense was an uncommon virtue." We all know people who do not learn from their mistakes. We are fortunate as Christians and should be encouraged by what James tells us in chapter one and verse five of his epistle. Not only does God want us to have a wisdom that He alone can provide and develop in us, He gives us the Scriptures and His Spirit to help. One of the most striking expressions in Scripture of humans being encouraged to rely on their good sense or judgment comes when Jesus sent out the twelve in Matthew 10:5-17.

> These twelve Jesus sent out with the following instructions: "Do not go among the Gentiles or enter any town of the Samaritans. Go rather to the lost sheep of Israel. You go, preach this message: 'The kingdom of heaven is near.' Heal the sick, raise the dead, cleanse those who have leprosy, drive out demons. Freely you have received, freely give. Do not take along any gold or silver or copper in your belts; take no bag for the journey, or extra

tunic, or sandals or a staff; for the worker is worth his keep. Whatever town or village you enter, search for some worthy person there and stay at his house until you leave. As you enter the home, give it your greeting. If the home is deserving, let your peace rest on it; if it is not, let your peace return to you. If anyone will not welcome you or listen to your words, shake the dust off your feet when you leave that home or town. I tell you the truth, it will be more bearable for Sodom and Gomorrah on the day of judgment than for that town. I am sending you out like sheep among wolves. Therefore be as shrewd as snakes and as innocent as doves."

Teach me knowledge and good judgment, for I believe in your commands.

Psalm 119:66

My son, preserve sound judgment and discernment, do not let them out of your sight.

Proverbs 3:21

A tyrannical ruler lacks judgment, but he who hates ill-gotten gain will enjoy a long life.

Proverbs 28:16

For by the grace given me I say to every one of you: Do not think of yourself more highly than you ought, but rather think of yourself with sober judgment, in accordance with the measure of faith God has given you.

Romans 12:3

If any of you lacks wisdom, he should ask God, who gives generously to all without finding fault, and it will be given to him.

James 1:5

But the wisdom that comes from heaven is first of all pure; then peace loving, considerate, submissive, full of mercy and good fruit, impartial and sincere.

James 3:17

CHAPTER 7

Actionable Faith

———— ❦ ————

One of the catch phrases to come out of the latest invasion of Iraq is "actionable intelligence" which means information that can be acted on. If we have a vast amount of information about our enemy, but don't use it purposefully, it is an unused encyclopedia. We can also have a faith in God that saves us, but that doesn't lead us to do anything else useful with it. My denomination has traditionally put a great emphasis on study. So great is that emphasis, some of our assemblies have a decidedly academic rather than worshipful or encouraging feel to them. James warns us that faith without works is dead. What we know and believe has to drive the things we do.

I have struggled to keep from putting faith and action into separate compartments in my life. I had the feeling that I was walking around in the real world and would have to stop what I was doing and consider the matter at hand from a godly perspective. I would seek the kingdom as though I was seeking the right tool to take out of my toolbox and use on the task at hand. That approach isn't necessarily wrong, but it certainly wasn't satisfying.

This reality of a pervasive kingdom of God lived out in our lives is consistent with what we read in Colossians 3:17: "Whatever you do, whether in word or deed, do it all in the name of the Lord Jesus, giving thanks to the Father through him."

How then do we keep from creating compartments in our lives and start putting our faith in God's authority into action? I came to Christ at the age of thirty-two and the Marine Corps way of life was so ingrained that it was difficult for me to keep from having a religion compartment in my life. Rather than recognizing the kingdom around me and the fact that I was now a part of that natural environment, I was using religion to manage sins and waiting for the biblical mission that would come along once I got my sin under control with God's help. Of course that's not like any model we see in the Bible of how God works with His people. He draws us to Him and establishes a loving relationship in which sin is put off like an old skin and the new creature is prepared to serve.

I was fully engaged, I was studying my Bible, praying, teaching the teenagers at church, attending retreats, and working at a church camp in the summer. I didn't curse as much and didn't tell the same stories as before, but when I put on the uniform it was in some ways putting back on the old skin.

I didn't realize the extent of the compartments in my life until I got a very literal wake up call at work one day. My clerk, Corporal Obendorfer, stuck his head in and told me someone was on the phone for me. I didn't want to talk to them so I told "OB" to tell them I wasn't there and to take a message. He obeyed, of course. It dawned on me that by doing what I'd always done, I was lying, forcing OB to lie, and sending out a very confusing message about the truth to my Marine brother. I called him in and told him that we had an integrity issue and if I ever did that again, he was to remind me that we couldn't lie. It was a humbling, but very necessary step in beginning to break down the compartments in my life.

To do everything in Jesus' name requires learning what He desires and finds acceptable. We have to read the words He has provided about Himself. Paul tells Timothy that scripture is God-breathed and the instrument for thoroughly equipping the man of God for every good work.[10] One of the ways we come to know God is by reading the Bible *and spending the time to really think about what we find there.* The Bible provides us with plenty of regulations, philosophy, and history—all useful elements that help us to be obedient and to know our place in the kingdom—but God also permits us insight into His person as we see His love letters to His people and the various accounts of His disappointment in us. When we combine all these elements with the words and actions of His Son, we have a clear picture of Him to whom we give our hearts in everything we do. Through His inspired Word, God provides us the

---

[10] 2 Timothy 3:16-17

framework for living our lives but does not provide specific direction for every situation in which we find ourselves. We as Christians have to translate what we read in conceptual form and convert it to concrete application in the changing circumstances of our individual lives.

Simply knowing the Scriptures is not enough; knowledge rightly applied becomes wisdom that prepares us to act more like Christ at every opportunity. We will need help along the way. An inexperienced second lieutenant is provided with a platoon sergeant, someone more experienced, who will help the lieutenant learn to think and operate like a Marine leader. The platoon sergeant can advise and encourage; the lieutenant, however, is still responsible for his or her decisions. In the same manner God provides a helper in the person of the Holy Spirit.[11] Unlike the fallible platoon sergeant, the Spirit knows perfectly the will and desires of the true Commander and will always help the Christian make the right decisions for God.

The good news for us as Christians is that God has given us a clear and uncomplicated path to gaining Godly wisdom—just ask for it. James makes this point clear in his extremely practical letter. He says, "If any of you lacks wisdom, he should ask God, who gives generously to all without finding fault, and it will be given to him."[12] Asking becomes the segue to the next requirement for being a Marine as though

---

[11] John 14:26

[12] James 1:5

we are working for the Lord. We must pray. Often, we approach prayer as a transaction or as a way to gain top cover for what we've already decided to do. Prayer needs to be conversation.

A trait we find in our best leaders is a sincere desire to talk to their Marines. During operations briefings our commanders will tell us what they expect and why it should be so. They will offer words of clarification and encouragement. One of the most anticipated times of communion with a commander (or feared, depending on the operation's outcome) is the after-action debrief or hot wash-up. A young Marine in the presence of a good commander will instinctively soak up every word uttered to better prepare for what is to come or to understand what they have experienced. Time spent with the experienced warrior is all the more rewarding when we are able to ask questions directly of the one in command. Very few Marines are fortunate enough to have a relationship that permits frequent contact with their commander. Incredibly enough, we as Christians have direct and open access to Almighty God through the blood of His Son, Jesus. The farther you are from frequent contact with the commander, the less likely his or her words are to have a significant impact on your routine actions. The same goes for the King of kings. If we choose not to read all we can about Him in inspired Scripture and choose not to pray, we can't expect to be complete in Him.

Having the commander's intent spelled out in our orders is also very helpful for choosing the correct course of action in a given situation, but nothing can replace having spent time in the field in a variety of situations to know first hand how the boss thinks and what he would expect from us.

To build self-reliance in their subordinates, good commanders will intentionally place them in situations where they have to think through the problem on their own. A Marine leader will draw on the experiences gained through contact with his or her commander and develop their own style of leadership and be successful. A Christian will draw on the experiences gained in trusting Christ and come to true success as they become Christ-like in all they do. In the first chapter of James we're told that trials test our faith; this testing produces perseverance and perseverance ultimately produces maturity and completeness.[13] The two verses together complete a picture of a mature Christian. In every trial we face, we persevere by choosing to remain in Christ and we build on our decisions and choices for Christ until we ultimately are relying on Him completely. We recognize a mature leader as one who can operate independently. A mature Christian, paradoxically, is one who has learned to rely, not on themselves, but on God. Jesus makes this point clearly when He says, "I am the vine; you are the branches. If a man remains in me and I in him, he will bear much fruit; apart from me you can do nothing."[14]

Here we have the picture of a Christian Marine who is earnestly seeking God: reading the Bible,

---

[13] James 1:2-4

[14] John 15:5

expectantly praying for godly wisdom, and remaining sensitive to the counsel of the Holy Spirit. This Marine's roots are sunk deep into godly soil and she is ready for action, prepared to rely on Christ when handling the challenges heading her way.

Knowledge: understanding of a science or an art. The range of one's information, including professional knowledge and an understanding of your Marines.

One of the first things a recruit or officer candidate is issued is a book of facts about the Marine Corps that he or she is expected to learn immediately. It's interesting that the book itself, even in its unopened state, is referred to in both camps as *knowledge*, as in, "Grab your *knowledge* and fall out for class." Memorization of general facts soon gives way to familiarity and understanding as a Marine or a new Christian gains experience on the path they have chosen. Learning doesn't stop in either walk. New aspects of long-known facts are revealed as they are revisited and reconsidered in the light of practical application.

Until we all reach unity in the faith and in the knowledge of the Son of God and become mature, attaining to the whole measure of the fullness of Christ.

Ephesians 4:13

And we pray this in order that you may live a life worthy of the Lord and may please him in every way: bearing fruit in every good work, growing in the knowledge of God.

Colossians 1:10

For this very reason, make every effort to add to your faith goodness; and to goodness, knowledge; and to knowledge, self-control; and to self-control, perseverance; and to perseverance, godliness; and to godliness, brotherly kindness; and to brotherly kindness, love. For if you possess these qualities in increasing measure, they will keep you from being ineffective and unproductive in of our Lord Jesus Christ.

2 Peter 1:5

But grow in the grace and knowledge of our Lord and Savior Jesus Christ.

2 Peter 3:18

For I can testify about them that they are zealous for God, but their zeal is not based on knowledge.

Romans 10:2

Decisiveness: the ability to make decisions promptly and to announce them in a clear, forceful manner.

We need to be thoughtful and prayerful people, not given to rash behavior we will regret later. But we have also been given a spirit of power, of love, and of self-discipline that permits us to act decisively when the situation requires it. Succumbing to fears and rationalization is no more a part of the Christian character than it is a part of the Marine Corps character. The decisiveness of a servant of God is born from the confidence in knowing what God would have us do. This doesn't mean that we should not take time to prayerfully consider our actions, but when we know what God would have us do, we must act on the knowledge He's given us of His ways and desires. I believe the story of David and his encounter with Goliath in 1 Samuel 17 is a tremendous example of decisiveness as defined above.

But no one announced his decision more clearly or forcefully than Joshua when he led the Israelites in renewing the covenant at Shechem. He said, "Now fear the LORD and serve him with all faithfulness. Throw away the gods your forefathers worshiped beyond the River and in Egypt, and serve the LORD. But if serving the LORD seems undesirable to you, then choose for yourselves this day whom you will serve, whether the gods your forefathers served beyond the River, or the gods of the Amorites, in whose land you are living. But as for me and my household, we will serve the LORD" (Joshua 24:15).

> Anyone, then, who knows the good he ought to do and doesn't do it, sins.
>
> James 4:17

> For God did not give us a spirit of timidity, but a spirit of power, of love and of self-discipline.
>
> 2 Timothy 1:7

> Even in the case of lifeless things that make sounds, such as the flute or harp, how will anyone know what tune is being played unless

there is a distinction in the notes? Again, if the trumpet does not sound a clear call, who will get ready for battle? So it is with you. Unless you speak intelligible words with your tongue, how will anyone know what you are saying? You will just be speaking into the air.

1 Corinthians 14:7-8

CHAPTER EIGHT

Faith in Action, Loving Your Neighbor Is Not for Sissies

J esus made it clear that the most important aspect of following God is to, "Love the Lord your God with all your heart and with all your soul and with all your mind. This is the first and greatest commandment." The Pharisee who was testing Him never got a chance to ask about another commandment because Jesus, without pausing included, "And the second is like it: 'Love your neighbor as yourself.' All the Law and the Prophets hang on these two commandments."[15] As we look to our vertical relationship, Jesus' words here make it clear that how we treat our fellow man is inextricably tied to how we love God.

---

[15] Matthew 22:34-40

If you ask most Marine leaders about "loving your neighbor," you are liable to get a furrowed brow and some meaningful squirming in response. Even a Marine who is a mature Christian will likely begin to qualify or clarify what loving a neighbor means to them. In a culture bred for war, this loving concept seems a little soft. But if you ask the same leaders how they feel about the Marines they led at some point in their career, especially the ones they led during combat or difficult operations, they will not hesitate to say, "Man, I loved those guys." As hard as it is to believe, loving your neighbor is, in fact, a Marine Corps tradition. I remember one occasion when I was a major and we had just wrapped up a big field exercise. We had just been told that we were staying in the field overnight because the commanding general wanted to address everyone. In the moment I allowed my cynicism to get the better of me and I told several of my officers that I could tell them what the CG was going to say and we could go ahead and get on the trucks right then. "Great exercise . . . broke new ground . . . important work." Sure enough, when "Spider" Nyland spoke that evening he said all those things. And then, after he'd pulled everyone in close, he said, "I'm proud of you, I love you guys." The tears in his eyes shamed me; I felt like the small man that I had acted like a few hours before. I can tell you that despite the emotion there was nothing soft about the general's words or feelings that afternoon.

When we teach our young Marines the leadership principles, no one gets uncomfortable when they hear "know your Marines and look out for their welfare." We don't get a queasy, soft feeling when we say, "Mission first, Marines always." But loving your neighbor seems just a little too maternal for us.

Who is my neighbor? From what we read in Jesus' response to this question in the parable of the good Samaritan, a simplified answer would be that your neighbor is someone who needs you, someone you can help. The man who had been beaten and robbed and left on the road to Jericho needed someone, anyone, to help him. As you look at the Marines you lead, it becomes clear that they need someone. If you are their leader, you are their neighbor. You may not be a perfect leader. You may be uncertain; you may even be too mission-oriented or selfish like the priest and the Levite who passed by the injured man on the Jericho road. But those Marines need you because you have been given the responsibility and authority to care for them.

They also need you because as human beings they have been robbed of the truth and beaten by the world they see around them, and you have been given the words of life from Christ. In addition to your Marines, you are called to be a neighbor to others you come in contact with. You may not have an official responsibility for them that is derived from regulations, but we are called to be a neighbor to everyone who doesn't know Christ.

To love our neighbors we have to overcome some discomfort and fears. I was a Marine for about ten years before I became a Christian. Even after I came to Christ I was very uncomfortable talking about my faith in the workplace. I was worried about being seen as abusing my authority and about having personal relationships that impinged on professional relationships. I have to admit truthfully that I was also somewhat embarrassed by what I expected other people's reactions to be when they found out I was a Christian. I was in a class once with an Air Force instructor who asked the question, "Are any of you born-again Christians?" I have to say that I did not raise my hand. For some reason I felt like I had to explain what kind of a Christian I was and defend myself before making an acknowledgement of my Christianity in front of people I did not know and could not have cared less about otherwise. My para-lyzed reaction was particularly ironic because the instructor was only making a reference to the fish symbol to make a point about symbols in general. Although I didn't go to the extreme that Peter did in the courtyard after Jesus' arrest, I nevertheless denied Him to whom I belonged. That has stuck with me. I was fully engaged in all Christian activities, I was studying my Bible, praying, teaching teen-agers at church, attending retreats, and working at a church camp in the summer. I didn't act differ-ently at work, but I was a silent partner with Christ. A real tension was building inside me; I felt like an undercover Christian. Jesus' words really bothered me: "Whoever acknowledges me before men, I will also acknowledge him before my Father in heaven. But whoever disowns me before men, I will disown him before my Father in heaven."[16] Even so, I didn't

---

[16] Matthew 10:31-33

want to be viewed as a Bible-thumper or some kind of nut. It wasn't until about five years after becoming a Christian that I got comfortable with whom I had become. The first and biggest step for me was just figuring out how to acknowledge Christ without being misunderstood. Of course, over time, God finally taught me that I was to acknowledge Him whether folks around me understood or not. Paul's words in Galatians 1:10 really convicted me: "Am I now trying to win the approval of men, or of God? Or am I trying to please men? If I were still trying to please men, I would not be a servant of Christ." The idea of not being Christ's servant made life very uncomfortable, but overcoming the desire to be well regarded by people around me was difficult. It took the second greatest commandment to finally break my reserve.

The wall between my faith and my works began to collapse when I was exercising my responsibility to care for my Marines. As a leader I dealt with many personal problems in their lives. Helping a Marine with a problem by arranging for Red Cross or Navy Relief support was a natural part of my duties. I found that it was also easy to overcome that spiritual reluctance when someone needed help. It was very natural to say, "I'll be praying for you" to a young person who was struggling with the loss of a grandparent or with a very sick parent. It took only the most minimal amount of courage at the hospital to ask if I could pray with one of my Marines for his sick daughter. I finally became comfortable in my relationship with Christ at work when I was talking to my Marines after the events of September 11, 2001. All our foundations were rocked that day and in the process of answering a question about the big picture, I found myself saying very naturally, "I'm a Christian, so I try to base the decisions I make on what I know of God." Once that water broke, I was confident in talking about my faith in Christ without embarrassment. That's not to say I do anything I should perfectly, but I was able to remove one of the walls that compartmented in my life—ten years after becoming a Christian!

The next step in putting my faith in action was harder and can still be difficult. Helping someone with physical needs or comforting someone in emotional distress can be relatively easy compared to helping with their spiritual needs, especially the ones who are hostile toward religion. Jesus said, "Go into all the world and tell the good news." But I didn't know enough, didn't have all the facts right. It would be nice to be able to say that I was worried about leading someone into error. But the truth is, once again, I was afraid of getting embarrassed. God taught me an important lesson when I was driving to a meeting with a co-worker one afternoon. My friend was older than me and had been divorced for a few years. She was really struggling with the betrayal and uncertainty. Our ride became very uncomfortable for me as she unburdened herself about being confused and bitter about her situation. While she was talking I was praying for something wise and helpful to say. She talked about being raised in the Catholic Church and turning away after she became an adult. She said that she had always tried to treat other people well and asked, "Isn't that what it's all about with God?" Once again I felt that familiar paralysis come over me. As I was on the verge of agreeing and changing the subject, God chose that time to answer my prayer to be helpful to her. The scripture from the greatest commandment came to mind. I told her that being good to other people certainly pleases God, but that caring for others was only half of the God story; the most important part is loving God completely. I explained that true caring for others around us wells up from a heart that focuses on God and recognizes how lost we are and in need of Him. It sounds very simple and basic as I relate it here, but it was a profound moment for me because through me, God had provided the answer to someone's questions about Him.

I invited her to church with me and told her we had several single ladies her age that I thought she would like. I know it would make a greater impact if I could conclude this story by saying she turned to Christ and everything worked out great for her. I think the truth is that this encounter was meant more for me than her. She probably doesn't remember it at all, but I do. It was the first time I really told anyone the Good News. The most important lesson I learned from this experience is that when I focus on myself and what I'm feeling and anticipating, I usually miss the mark. If I get my ego out of the way and let God speak, there is never a failure, even when we can't see a successful outcome from our point of view.

Knowing that you are representing Christ through your words and actions should cause you to act more like Him in all circumstances. Do not be reluctant to take care of your Marines' physical and emotional needs. A cup of cold water to help out and words of comfort will be natural outpourings from the depth of your relationship with God. Be prepared and willing to help them with their spiritual needs.

The real watershed in my walk with God came during our time in Okinawa when I stepped out in faith and really began to love my neighbor. Until that time I had never met anyone who was contemplating suicide. I had attended all the mandatory training and was aware of the ins and outs of dealing with suicidal behavior, but nothing in the classes prepared me to deal with real people who were so despondent they didn't want to live. One Marine worked for me and another who came along later was a member of my congregation. I watched them both get inducted into the military mental health system, hospitalized, counseled, and ultimately discharged from the service. Both of these men (boys, really) had deeper emotional problems than were apparent on the surface and they needed more than the system was able to provide. I have to say that it wasn't easy dealing with these guys, especially the fellow Christian. I was a senior officer spending time in the hospital with a lance corporal, talking to his first sergeant and getting personally involved in his life. I tried to keep the arm's length between us that I knew was best from the Marine point of view, but he was so damaged, so depressed, that it was hard to do so. Like most men, I felt I should be fixing the problem, that the long sessions of talking should lead to some solution, but I also knew that was unrealistic, given his state of mind. Talking to him was exhausting at times as his moods swung from elation to despair. After a while I would begin to make excuses for not checking up on him just to get some distance. But whenever I made the excuses God would gently convict me all over again and I couldn't resist trying to help even though it seemed to do no good. I did learn the practical value of relying on the Bible to get someone to focus somewhere other than themselves. I am no Bible scholar and must rely heavily on a concordance to find the scripture I'm looking for, but the right words came at the right time to help. Although I didn't fix anything in my brother's life, I was there so he was not alone during the lowest times and we were able to keep God front and center at a time when he wouldn't have been able to do it himself, but needed it most. Looking back, it's clear that God was also using that time with my friend to teach me and show me the deeper meaning of things of His kingdom.

It is no accident that you are where you are. Your leadership in combat or force protection efforts may save the lives of Marines. Your spiritual leadership may play a part in saving eternal lives in Christ. Teach Bible classes or lead devotional discussions to those who wish to attend, especially during combat, time in the field, or on deployment.

Is it possible to maintain the professional distance that leadership requires if you involve yourself in the spiritual lives of the Marines you lead and those around you? What problems may arise? First, young Marines may become confused by your spiritual interest. Secondly, some may seek to exploit a personal relationship. This usually is not the case with Marines; they normally maintain a healthy respect for differences in rank. The third problem may arise when your actions are criticized by outside observers. Some people with an ingrained prejudice against Christians may criticize you regardless of the propriety of your actions. Remember where your first loyalty lies and that blessing comes with insult because of your service to Christ. "Blessed are you when people insult you, persecute you and falsely say all kinds of evil against you because of me. Rejoice and be glad, because great is your reward in heaven, for in the same way they persecuted the prophets who were before you."[17]

It is important to begin spiritual involvement with individuals as you intend to continue. Don't get too informal or set improper parameters for dealing with Marines' spiritual needs, especially for the ones you lead directly. If you sincerely seek the will of God and jealously guard your integrity in every aspect of your relationships with others, there should be no conflict. If Cornelius and other Roman centurions were able to serve Christ, so can you. Trust the Holy Spirit to lead you.

At some point you may have to decide between serving God and serving as a Marine. If your desire to preach or conduct Bible studies is so overwhelming that you feel you must do it on company time,

---

[17] Matthew 5:11-12

you may need to check your motivation. You may be driven by pride rather than obedience. I'm not recommending backing away from what we are all called to be, but our contending for the faith needs to remain in balance with our respect for the authorities appointed over us, and respect for the people we are trying to reach.

> But even if you should suffer for what is right, you are blessed. "Do not fear what they fear; do not be frightened." But in your hearts set apart Christ as Lord. Always be prepared to give an answer to everyone who asks you to give the reason for the hope that you have. But do this with gentleness and respect, keeping a clear conscience, so that those who speak maliciously against your good behavior in Christ may be ashamed of their slander.
>
> 1 Peter 3:14-16

A humble desire to serve as a Marine and as an ambassador for Jesus will keep your actions on the straight and narrow path. You may be called to suffer the consequences for making a stand for the truth; many Christians have. Just make sure your intent is pure and that you aren't seeking glory for yourself, rather than for the One who is worthy.

Endurance: the mental and physical stamina measured by the ability to withstand pain, fatigue, stress, and hardship.

The Bible speaks of endurance so often that one might be tempted to think the Christian life is one long chore to be trudged through. The earlier Christians certainly had plenty of trudging to do. In addition to the same trials of self-denial we commonly face today, they were persecuted by Roman and secular authorities as well as the Jewish leaders of their day. It might be easy to think of the Christian life as one long effort to hang in there until we get to heaven, but that's not accurate. For every instance of endurance, Scripture speaks more than ten times of *joy*. Similarly, for a Marine, endurance is part of life, but the satisfaction and pride of being a Marine outweighs that which has to be endured.

> For everything that was written in the past was written to teach us, so that through endurance and the encouragement of the Scriptures we might have hope. May the God who gives endurance and encouragement give you a spirit of unity among yourselves as you follow Christ Jesus.
>
> Romans 15:4-5

> Rather, as servants of God we commend ourselves in every way: in great endurance; in troubles, hardships and distresses.
>
> 2 Corinthians 6:4

We continually remember before our God and Father your work produced by faith, your labor prompted by love, and your endurance inspired by hope in our Lord Jesus Christ.

1 Thessalonians 1:3

Endure hardship with us like a good soldier of Christ Jesus.

2 Timothy 2:3

If we endure, we will also reign with him. If we disown him, he will also disown us.

2 Timothy 2:12

Consider him who endured such opposition from sinful men, so that you will not grow weary and lose heart.

Hebrews 12:3

Endure hardship as discipline; God is treating you as sons. For what son is not disciplined by his father?

Hebrews 12:7

Unselfishness: avoidance of providing for one's own comfort and personal advancement at the expense of others.

I have always loved to eat, even chow hall food. In the field hot chow was always one of the best parts of the day. I have also always hated to be cold. The memory of January on the DMZ in Korea still sets me on edge. When I became an officer I was taught a couple of Marine traditions that make great common sense for leaders, but which I found nearly unbearable at times. The first is the practice of putting your Marines ahead of you in the chow line, and the second is wearing only issued cold weather gear since you should be wearing what your Marines wear so you can accurately gauge the effects of the cold on them. It was especially hard in the days before Goretex and polypro. These minor examples of unselfishness were somewhat difficult to bear. Even harder to bear at times is unselfishness that Christ requires of His followers. His requirements go beyond unselfishness and into the realm of self-denial. He gave us the ultimate example of unselfishness when He took our place on the cross, although He in no way deserved it. Of all the characters in the Bible, Uriah the Hittite directly epitomizes the military definition of unselfishness and putting our Marines' welfare ahead of our own. Although he did not know it, his selflessness and loyalty to his comrades in arms would lead directly to his death.[18]

> Do nothing out of selfish ambition or vain conceit, but in humility consider others better than yourselves. Each of you should look not only to your own interests, but also to the interests of others.
>
> Philippians 2:3

---

[18] 2 Samuel 11

Then Jesus said to his disciples, "If anyone would come after me, he must deny himself and take up his cross and follow me."

Matthew 16:24

But if you harbor bitter envy and selfish ambition in your hearts, do not boast about it or deny the truth.

James 3:14

Initiative: taking action in the absence of orders.

Taking initiative requires a certain amount of knowledge about what needs to be done, as well as sound judgment in selecting a course of action, and the confidence to begin. In the Corps we have our values and training to draw from as we begin to take action. We may also have our commander's intent to guide us when orders are not forthcoming. We have the same resources in our walk with God and the added resources of prayer and the presence of the Holy Spirit to help guide us. A wise friend of mine named Fred Zumwalt has observed that sometimes we spend time in prayer asking for guidance and waiting for direction when the answer to what we should be doing is already abundantly clear just from what we know of God's character and His desires by reading the Bible.

Anyone, then, who knows the good he ought to do and doesn't do it, sins.

James 4:17

In the same way, faith by itself, if it is not accompanied by action, is dead.

James 2:17

For Titus not only welcomed our appeal, but he is coming to you with much enthusiasm and on his own initiative.

2 Corinthians 8:17

Again, it will be like a man going on a journey, who called his servants and entrusted his property to them. To one he gave five talents of money, to another two talents, and to another one talent, each according to his ability. Then he went on his journey. The man who had received the five talents went at once and put his money to work and gained five more. So also, the one with the two talents gained two more. But the man who had received the one talent went off, dug a hole in the ground and hid his master's money. After a long time the master of those servants returned and settled accounts with them. The man who had received the five talents brought the other five. "Master," he said, "you entrusted me with five talents. See, I have gained five more." His master replied, "Well done, good and faithful servant! You have been faithful with a few things; I will put you in charge of many things. Come and share your master's happiness!"

Matthew 25:14-21

Then the eleven disciples went to Galilee, to the mountain where Jesus told them to go. When they saw him, they worshiped him; but some doubted. Then Jesus came to them and said, "All authority in heaven and on earth has been given to me. Therefore go and make disciples of all nations, baptizing them in the name of the Father and of the Son and of the Holy Spirit, and teaching them to obey everything I have commanded you. And surely I am with you always, to the very end of the age."

Matthew 28:18-20

Appendix: Questions for Consideration and Discussion

Chapter One
Uriah, the First Marine

2 Samuel 11
Where should David have been that spring and why?
In what ways did Uriah demonstrate courage?
Whom did Uriah honor and how did he demonstrate honor?
How did Uriah demonstrate commitment?

Lesson Two
Semper Fidelis and the Greatest Commandment

Matthew 22:34-38
Contrast the Marine Corps motto with what we see in

modern American culture.

To what are Marines called to be faithful?

Is that different from other services?

How will our lives be different if we take the greatest commandment at face value with no caveats or analysis?

What do we think would be the outcome of taking it at face value?

Chapter Three
Who Better to Carry Out the Great Commission?

Matthew 28:18-20
Discuss military life in light of the elements we see in the Great Commission:
- authority
- therefore go
- make disciples
- obey

Which scriptures come to mind when we consider each of these four elements of the Great Commission?

Chapter Four
Can a Marine Really Be a Christian and Vice Versa?

Matthew 8:5-13
Acts Chapter 10
What is Jesus' attitude toward the centurion at Capernaum?

Why is Cornelius such an important character in biblical history?

What conclusions can be drawn from the examples of the two centurions?

What conclusions might we draw incorrectly by overstating the significance of the centurions?

What is the legal status of Christians in the military?

Chapter Five
Pure Religion in the Barracks

James 1:26-27

Is Christianity fair?

How far should tolerance and respect for diversity extend?

On what should we base our views of others who believe differently?

How does the pollution we find in the barracks differ from the pollution we find in the rest of the world?

Consider the contrast between breaking the law or a regulation and bringing dishonor to oneself as a Marine, and separately, as a Christian.

Chapter Six
Idolatry in the Ranks

Exodus 20:3

What do Marines worship?

Do you know anyone who was redeemed by the Corps?

Where does self-respect end and destructive pride begin?

How can traditions be worshipped?

Chapter Seven
Actionable Faith

James 1:1-27
How does faith and works (or action) interrelate?
Is there a Christian equivalent for commander's intent?
Are you comfortable with the idea of prayer as two-way communication?
How can knowledge be a double-edged sword?

Chapter Eight
Faith in Action, Loving Your Neighbors Is Not for Sissies

Matthew 22:34-40
What tension exists between loving our neighbors and Marine Corps culture?
What fears do we need to overcome in this regard?
What elements exist within Marine Corps culture that are natural extensions of loving our neighbor?
Give some examples of how Marines love their neighbor.
How can we retain good order and discipline across rank and leadership gulfs as we try to help other Marines?

Printed in the United States
84926LV00001B/100-195/A